radical
kindness

jesus every day
Devotional Guide

CANDACE | DaySpring

candacecbure.com | dayspring.com

Welcome!

I'm thrilled that you've picked up this book so we can study one of my favorite topics: *kindness.*

Kindness is powerful. It unleashes God's love toward others in ways that can radically restore relationships and transform lives. But kindness doesn't just happen naturally. We have to intentionally seek to practice it and learn how we can better show it.

The Bible is filled with examples of God's unmerited kindness toward His people. In fact, God delights in being kind to us. Jeremiah 31:3 says God draws us "with unfailing kindness" (NIV). He wants us to imitate Him by being kind to others and to ourselves.

The Bible readings in this devotional guide demonstrate the transforming power of kindness. They will help you learn more about who God is and His desire for us to selflessly and radically love others through acts of kindness.

You won't always see how your kindness affects others. But God sees your heart, and you'll never regret showing someone the same kind of radical kindness that God has shown you.

In this together, *Candace*

Before You Get Started on This Adventure

*H*ere's the deal. You're picking this book up and are either super excited to dig in or wondering if you really want to start this journey with me. I get it. Trust me, I do. And while I can tell you that this study can undoubtedly change your life, you may not be eager to jump in based on my enthusiasm alone. But would you do me a favor? Would you at least read through this first section before you put this book back on the shelf?

Before jumping into it, you might be wondering why the Bible is worth reading or what all the talk about being "saved" means. You may feel like you'll never measure up to God's standards—that there's no hope for you—so why even try? Or maybe you feel like you're doing just fine and life is actually pretty good, so why would you need to dig deep into God's Word?

Wherever you are in your spiritual journey, I want you to know you're not alone. In this first section, I've answered some questions people typically ask me about my Christian faith. I hope these answers will be helpful to you too.

Why should I read and study the Bible?

The world is full of all kinds of books that tell stories, teach concepts, inspire, and entertain. Heck, I've even written a few of them! Many books have influenced the world throughout history, but none compare with the Bible.

We all love a good story, right? While the Bible is full of history, wisdom, guidelines, and poetry, it's actually the epic story about all of creation and time from the beginning to the end. In the Bible, God is the ultimate storyteller—He shares His plan, His story, and His design for the world and for humanity.

The story begins with God creating His beloved humanity—Adam and Eve—in His image. But they destroyed their relationship with Him by choosing power instead of trusting in Him. Then the rest of the Bible—the greatest love story ever told—continues as God sets His plan in motion to bring His people back to Himself.

While there are other books that claim to be "holy," and even some that may contain useful ideas or wise words, no other book explains so clearly humanity's desperate need for rescue and how God Himself came to the rescue by sending His only Son, Jesus. No other book is so transformational because no other book shows us how much we are *loved* by our Creator.

What does it mean to be "saved"?

When followers of Jesus talk about being saved, we mean that Jesus rescued us from the ultimate consequence of sin—eternal separation from God—and our lives are no longer controlled by sin or filled with darkness, hopelessness, shame, guilt, and fear.

Jesus shines His light, freedom, joy, peace, and hope into our lives. God doesn't want sin to have any control over us. He wants to have a relationship with us. He wants us to live full, abundant, joyful lives that reflect His goodness back to others! That's why Jesus came—to save us from the punishment we deserve because of our sin and to give us new life.

Being saved doesn't mean we are spared from all suffering in our lives. But it does mean we have God's presence with us and the promise of spending forever with Him— an eternity free from all pain and suffering. Jesus is ready to save us the moment we open our hearts to Him and accept His unconditional love for us.

What if I don't need to be "saved"?

I get this too—you're a good person, you help others, you live honestly, you probably donate time and money to charity, and you're not hurting anyone. Why do you need to be "saved"? Compared to others, you're practically a saint! But God's standards are different from human standards. If we just compare ourselves to other people, it's easy to think we're good enough. But when we compare ourselves to God's standards, we fall miserably short. Every. Single. Time.

We all deserve God's judgment. Because He is holy, He cannot allow sin anywhere near Him. Because of sin, we cannot earn our way to having a relationship with God. Our sin separates us from our Creator. God says that if we break even one commandment, it's as if we're guilty of breaking them all. There isn't one of us who can say we are sinless. And doing good things to earn God's approval doesn't erase our sinfulness either. But because God loves us, He sent His Son, Jesus, to die so that all people—the bad, the good, and everyone in between—could have a relationship with Him.

$\mathcal{B}$ecause I believe the Bible shows us who Jesus is and how we can have a relationship with Him, I want to help you get to know Him too. That's what this study guide is all about.

How do I use this study guide?

Here's how it works: each day has a reading from the Bible and then some questions to help you think about and apply the biblical concepts. It's that simple! There's no "right" answer, and you can add your own questions and thoughts at any point, on any page.

Ideally, this is a personal journey where God will speak directly to your heart. But going through the study with friends can bring you encouragement and help you connect with others in really valuable ways. If you'd like, you could complete a day's study alone and then come together with a group of friends to discuss what God is showing you. You decide!

Let's do this!

As you go through each day's study, pray through it. Don't just complete it so you can check it off your to-do list. And don't look to me to tell you the answers or what to think; look to the Word and ask God to speak to you. Lastly, don't be afraid. The most repeated command in the Bible is "Do not fear," and one of the most common promises from God is "I am with you." So jump into this adventure and ask God what He wants to reveal to you.

Whether you are new to the Bible or super familiar with it, I can tell you this: God's Word is living and active. It will bring you life, and you will thrive every day as you find truth, peace, and hope within its pages. Let's go!

Kindness Is Accepting

LUKE 19:1–10 (CSB)

[Jesus] entered Jericho and was passing through. There was a man named Zacchaeus who was a chief tax collector, and he was rich. He was trying to see who Jesus was, but he was not able because of the crowd, since he was a short man. So running ahead, he climbed up a sycamore tree to see Jesus, since He was about to pass that way. When Jesus came to the place, He looked up and said to him, "Zacchaeus, hurry and come down because today it is necessary for Me to stay at your house."

So he quickly came down and welcomed Him joyfully. All who saw it began to complain, "He's gone to stay with a sinful man."

But Zacchaeus stood there and said to the Lord, "Look, I'll give half of my possessions to the poor, Lord. And if I have extorted anything from anyone, I'll pay back four times as much."

"Today salvation has come to this house," Jesus told him, "because he too is a son of Abraham. For the Son of Man has come to seek and to save the lost."

How easy or difficult is it for you to show kindness and acceptance to someone who is behaving in an unloving way toward you or others? Why?

In the time of Jesus, tax collectors were scorned and hated because they commonly practiced extortion. What does it say about Jesus that He would stop and talk to such a greedy person?

How did Jesus' kindness toward Zacchaeus change Zacchaeus's heart?

A LITTLE BIT OF

KINDNESS

MAKES A

BIG

DIFFERENCE.

We all know people whose values and actions differ from our own.

How do your actions toward those people reflect the actions of Jesus toward Zacchaeus?

In what ways do your behaviors and attitudes need to align more with those of Jesus?

_____

_____

_____

_____

_____

_____

_____

_____

_____

_____

_____

_____

_____

A NOTE FROM CANDACE

Jesus showed kindness to all people, despite their sinfulness. There's a difference between acceptance and affirmation. As a Christian, I can accept people without affirming everything they are doing. Accepting them means I want them to have a relationship with Jesus Christ, and then He'll take it from there.

Kindness Is Classy

Acts 9:36–43 (NLT)

There was a believer in Joppa named Tabitha (which in Greek is Dorcas). She was always doing kind things for others and helping the poor. About this time she became ill and died. Her body was washed for burial and laid in an upstairs room. But the believers had heard that Peter was nearby at Lydda, so they sent two men to beg him, "Please come as soon as possible!"

So Peter returned with them; and as soon as he arrived, they took him to the upstairs room. The room was filled with widows who were weeping and showing him the coats and other clothes Dorcas had made for them. But Peter asked them all to leave the room; then he knelt and prayed. Turning to the body he said, "Get up, Tabitha." And she opened her eyes! When she saw Peter, she sat up! He gave her his hand and helped her up. Then he called in the widows and all the believers, and he presented her to them alive.

The news spread through the whole town, and many believed in the Lord. And Peter stayed a long time in Joppa, living with Simon, a tanner of hides.

How would you describe someone who is classy (you may want to

look up the definition of **classy** *in the dictionary)?*

How does Luke (the author of the book of Acts) describe Tabitha?

How is she classy—in other words, how is she admirable, skillful, and full of grace?

How did followers of Jesus respond to Tabitha's death?

And how did many people in the town respond to her miraculous resurrection?

WHOEVER PURSUES RIGHTEOUSNESS AND KINDNESS WILL FIND

LIFE,

RIGHTEOUSNESS,

AND

HONOR.

— PROVERBS 21:21 (ESV)

Who are the people in your life that you admire because of their classy kindness?

How are they like Tabitha? How would other people describe your acts of kindness?

_____
_____
_____
_____
_____
_____
_____
_____
_____
_____
_____
_____
_____
_____

YOUR BIGGEST TAKEAWAY

Kindness Reveals God's Heart

ISAIAH 63:7—9 (NIV)

I will tell of the kindnesses of the LORD,
   the deeds for which He is to be praised,
   according to all the LORD has done for us—
yes, the many good things
   He has done for Israel,
   according to His compassion and many kindnesses.
He said, "Surely they are My people,
   children who will be true to Me";
   and so He became their Savior.
In all their distress He too was distressed,
   and the angel of His presence saved them.
In His love and mercy He redeemed them;
   He lifted them up and carried them
   all the days of old.

How do you like to share good news with other people?

According to this passage, how does God feel about His people, and how does He treat them?

In these verses, the prophet Isaiah tells us that God "is to be praised" because of His compassionate and kind deeds. How do you respond to God's love and care for you?

For His
MERCIFUL KINDNESS
is great
toward us.

— Psalm 117:2 (nkjv)

Reflect on the words "I will tell of the kindnesses of the LORD." In what ways have you experienced God's kindness, and how can you share what He's done in your life with other people?

_____

_____

_____

_____

_____

_____

_____

_____

_____

_____

_____

_____

_____

_____

YOUR BIGGEST TAKEAWAY

Kindness Is Powerful

I Samuel 25:4—33 (NLT)

[David and his men had shown kindness to the shepherds of a man named Nabal. When David asked Nabal if he would share provisions with David and his men, Nabal rudely insulted them and refused to give them anything. David immediately gathered his men—with their swords—and headed out to take revenge on Nabal. Meanwhile, Nabal's wife, Abigail, heard how her husband had mistreated David and his men.]

Abigail wasted no time. She quickly gathered 200 loaves of bread, two wineskins full of wine, five sheep that had been slaughtered, nearly a bushel of roasted grain, 100 clusters of raisins, and 200 fig cakes. She packed them on donkeys and said to her servants, "Go on ahead. I will follow you shortly." But she didn't tell her husband Nabal what she was doing. . . .

When Abigail saw David, she quickly got off her donkey and bowed low before him. She fell at his feet and said, "I accept all blame in this matter, my lord. . . . Here is a present that I, your servant, have brought to you and your young men. . . . When the LORD has done all He promised and has made you leader of Israel, don't let this be a blemish on your record." . . .

David replied to Abigail, "Praise the LORD, the God of Israel, who has sent you to meet me today! Thank God for your good sense! Bless you for keeping me from murder and from carrying out vengeance with my own hands."

*For more on the kindness of Abigail, read I Samuel 25:2—42.

Describe a time when someone's act of kindness radically changed your attitude or your behavior. How did the person's kindness affect your view of that person?

In this story, how did Abigail's kindness powerfully change David's course of action?

What is David's response to Abigail in this story?

KINDNESS
IS THE NOBLEST
WEAPON
TO CONQUER WITH.

— THOMAS FULLER

Think about a person in your life who may need an intervention of kindness.

Perhaps you know someone who is consumed with bitterness or thoughts of revenge.

How can you powerfully demonstrate God's love to that person this week?

_____

_____

_____

_____

_____

_____

_____

_____

_____

_____

_____

_____

A NOTE FROM CANDACE

The power in kindness is often missed or misunderstood—especially when people who consistently show kindness are misjudged as being "nice" or weak. But kindness is not for pushovers. It's strong, courageous, purposeful, and life changing.

Kindness Takes Courage

I Kings 17:7–16 (ESV)

There was no rain in the land. Then the word of the LORD came to [Elijah], "Arise, go to Zarephath, which belongs to Sidon, and dwell there. Behold, I have commanded a widow there to feed you." So he arose and went to Zarephath. And when he came to the gate of the city, behold, a widow was there gathering sticks. And he called to her and said, "Bring me a little water in a vessel, that I may drink." And as she was going to bring it, he called to her and said, "Bring me a morsel of bread in your hand." And she said, "As the LORD your God lives, I have nothing baked, only a handful of flour in a jar and a little oil in a jug. And now I am gathering a couple of sticks that I may go in and prepare it for myself and my son, that we may eat it and die." And Elijah said to her, "Do not fear; go and do as you have said. But first make me a little cake of it and bring it to me, and afterward make something for yourself and your son. For thus says the LORD, the God of Israel, 'The jar of flour shall not be spent, and the jug of oil shall not be empty, until the day that the LORD sends rain upon the earth.'" And she went and did as Elijah said. And she and he and her household ate for many days. The jar of flour was not spent, neither did the jug of oil become empty, according to the word of the LORD that he spoke by Elijah.

Describe a time when being kind to someone required you to act courageously.

How does the widow in this story demonstrate incredible courage?

How does God provide for Elijah in this story? How does God provide for the widow and her son?

KINDNESS

CAN OVERCOME

FEAR.

What does this story teach you about God and the ways He provides for people?

How has He provided for you in unexpected ways?

_____

_____

_____

_____

_____

_____

_____

_____

_____

_____

_____

_____

_____

_____

YOUR BIGGEST TAKEAWAY

DAY 6

Kindness Is Unexpected

31

Joshua 2:1–15; 6:25 (CSB)

[Joshua, the leader of the Israelites, sent two men to scout the land God had promised to them. They went to the city of Jericho and stayed at the house of a prostitute named Rahab. The king of Jericho heard about the Israelite spies and sent men to Rahab's house. But Rahab had hidden the spies under stalks of flax on her roof. She told the men from Jericho that the Israelite men had left at nightfall, so they left to chase after them.] Before the men fell asleep, she went up on the roof and said to them, "I know that the LORD has given you this land and that the terror of you has fallen on us, and everyone who lives in the land is panicking because of you. . . . Now please swear to me by the LORD that you will also show kindness to my father's family, because I showed kindness to you. Give me a sure sign that you will spare the lives of my father, mother, brothers, sisters, and all who belong to them, and save us from death."

The men answered her, "We will give our lives for yours. If you don't report our mission, we will show kindness and faithfulness to you when the LORD gives us the land."

Then she let them down by a rope through the window, since she lived in a house that was built into the wall of the city. . . .

[Later, when the Israelites conquered Jericho,] Joshua spared Rahab the prostitute, her father's family, and all who belonged to her, because she hid the messengers Joshua had sent to spy on Jericho.

How have you experienced kindness in unexpected ways or by

someone who surprised you by their actions?

What unexpected details and acts of kindness are evident

in the story of Rahab and the Israelite spies?

What motivated Rahab's kindness to the Israelite spies?

KINDNESS
FLOWS FROM A
FAITH-FILLED
HEART.

The Bible tells us that Rahab was saved because of her faith in God

(if you have time, read Hebrews 11:31 and James 2:25).

She became an ancestor of Jesus! How does the story of Rahab encourage you?

_____

_____

_____

_____

_____

_____

_____

_____

_____

_____

_____

_____

_____

YOUR BIGGEST TAKEAWAY

Kindness Leads to Common Ground

ACTS 28:1–10 (NIV)

[Paul and other prisoners being taken to Rome are shipwrecked.] Once safely on shore, we found out that the island was called Malta. The islanders showed us unusual kindness. They built a fire and welcomed us all because it was raining and cold. Paul gathered a pile of brushwood and, as he put it on the fire, a viper, driven out by the heat, fastened itself on his hand. When the islanders saw the snake hanging from his hand, they said to each other, "This man must be a murderer; for though he escaped from the sea, the goddess Justice has not allowed him to live." But Paul shook the snake off into the fire and suffered no ill effects. The people expected him to swell up or suddenly fall dead; but after waiting a long time and seeing nothing unusual happen to him, they changed their minds and said he was a god.

There was an estate nearby that belonged to Publius, the chief official of the island. He welcomed us to his home and showed us generous hospitality for three days. His father was sick in bed, suffering from fever and dysentery. Paul went in to see him and, after prayer, placed his hands on him and healed him. When this had happened, the rest of the sick on the island came and were cured. They honored us in many ways; and when we were ready to sail, they furnished us with the supplies we needed.

When have you been faced with a decision to either walk away from someone you

feel uncomfortable around or offer that person something they needed?

In this story from Acts, Paul and other prisoners suffered a shipwreck and ended up on an island.

How do the islanders treat the prisoners? How does Paul show kindness to people of Malta?

How does kindness in this story create common ground

between two vastly different groups of people?

BE KIND

AND

COMPASSIONATE

TO ONE ANOTHER.

— EPHESIANS 4:32

What surprises you about this story? How can you be intentional this

week in showing kindness to people who are different from you?

_____

_____

_____

_____

_____

_____

_____

_____

_____

_____

_____

_____

_____

_____

A NOTE FROM CANDACE

One day when I was on *The View,* I received terrifying news about an active shooter in my children's school district. A cohost comforted me and offered me her support. Even though we share dynamically different views, her kindness to me created common ground between us.

Kindness
Is Loyal

II SAMUEL 9:2—10 (ESV)

[David's closest friend, Jonathan, was the son of Israel's King Saul, who had attempted to murder David on numerous occasions (see I Samuel 18–19; 24; 26). After Saul and Jonathan died, David wanted to show his loyalty to Jonathan.] There was a servant of the house of Saul whose name was Ziba, and they called him to David. . . . And the king said, "Is there not still someone of the house of Saul, that I may show the kindness of God to him?" Ziba said to the king, "There is still a son of Jonathan; he is crippled in his feet." The king said to him, "Where is he?" And Ziba said to the king, "He is in the house of Machir the son of Ammiel, at Lo-debar." Then King David sent and brought him from the house of Machir the son of Ammiel, at Lo-debar. And Mephibosheth the son of Jonathan, son of Saul, came to David and fell on his face and paid homage. And David said, "Mephibosheth!" And he answered, "Behold, I am your servant." And David said to him, "Do not fear, for I will show you kindness for the sake of your father Jonathan, and I will restore to you all the land of Saul your father, and you shall eat at my table always." And he paid homage and said, "What is your servant, that you should show regard for a dead dog such as I?"

Then the king called Ziba, Saul's servant, and said to him, "All that belonged to Saul and to all his house I have given to your master's grandson. And you and your sons and your servants shall till the land for him and shall bring in the produce, that your master's grandson may have bread to eat. But Mephibosheth your master's grandson shall always eat at my table."

What relationships in your life are characterized by loyalty?

What does this story tell you about David's friendship with Jonathan, Saul's son?

How does Mephibosheth respond to David when David honors him?

Why does he respond this way?

NEVER LET
LOYALTY
AND
KINDNESS
LEAVE YOU!

— PROVERBS 3:3 (NLT)

In what ways have you experienced kindness from others because of their loyalty to someone close to you? How have you demonstrated loyalty through your acts of kindness to others?

YOUR BIGGEST TAKEAWAY

45

Kindness Demonstrates Jesus' Love

II Corinthians 5:14–21 (NLT)

Christ's love controls us. Since we believe that Christ died for all, we also believe that we have all died to our old life. He died for everyone so that those who receive His new life will no longer live for themselves. Instead, they will live for Christ, who died and was raised for them.

So we have stopped evaluating others from a human point of view. At one time we thought of Christ merely from a human point of view. How differently we know Him now! This means that anyone who belongs to Christ has become a new person. The old life is gone; a new life has begun!

And all of this is a gift from God, who brought us back to Himself through Christ. And God has given us this task of reconciling people to Him. For God was in Christ, reconciling the world to Himself, no longer counting people's sins against them. And He gave us this wonderful message of reconciliation. So we are Christ's ambassadors; God is making His appeal through us. We speak for Christ when we plead, "Come back to God!" For God made Christ, who never sinned, to be the offering for our sin, so that we could be made right with God through Christ.

Think about the person who first introduced you to Jesus.

How would you describe that person?

According to these verses, what has God done for us through His Son, Jesus Christ?

How does knowing Jesus directly influence how we view other people and how we treat them?

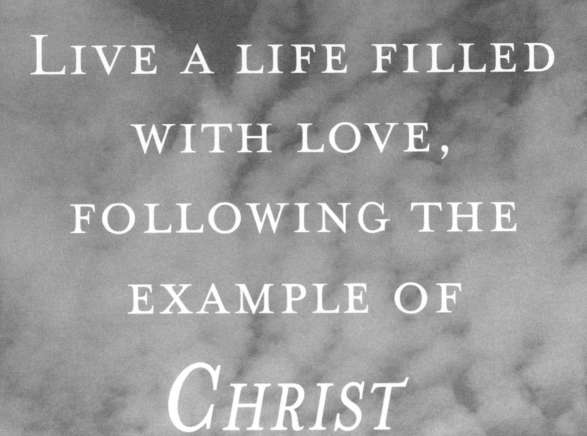

LIVE A LIFE FILLED
WITH LOVE,
FOLLOWING THE
EXAMPLE OF
CHRIST

— PSALM 138:8 (NLT)

In these verses, the author, Paul, wrote that "we are Christ's ambassadors."

In what ways can you lovingly represent Christ to other people?

_____

_____

_____

_____

_____

_____

_____

_____

_____

_____

_____

_____

_____

YOUR BIGGEST TAKEAWAY

DAY 10

Kindness
Is Selfless

JOHN 12:1—8 (CEV)

Six days before Passover Jesus went back to Bethany, where He had raised Lazarus from death. A meal had been prepared for Jesus. Martha was doing the serving, and Lazarus himself was there.

Mary took a very expensive bottle of perfume and poured it on Jesus' feet. She wiped them with her hair, and the sweet smell of the perfume filled the house.

A disciple named Judas Iscariot was there. He was the one who was going to betray Jesus, and he asked, "Why wasn't this perfume sold for three hundred silver coins and the money given to the poor?" Judas did not really care about the poor. He asked this because he carried the moneybag and sometimes would steal from it.

Jesus replied, "Leave her alone! She has kept this perfume for the day of My burial. You will always have the poor with you, but you won't always have Me."

What selfless act of kindness have you recently witnessed?

What is so unusual about what Mary does for Jesus? Why does it bother Judas?

In His response to Judas, Jesus wasn't saying that it's not important to care for poor people. Rather, Jesus knew He would soon die on the cross, and He welcomed Mary's humble and costly act of devotion. What can you learn from this story about how Jesus sees our motives and priorities?

SERVE ONE ANOTHER HUMBLY IN *LOVE.*

— GALATIANS 5:13 (NIV)

Our love for Jesus should compel us to put Him first

in our lives and selflessly serve Him—no matter the cost.

How are you actively showing your love for Jesus without expecting anything in return?

_____

_____

_____

_____

_____

_____

_____

_____

_____

_____

_____

_____

_____

_____

A NOTE FROM CANDACE

Many people don't understand the concept of choosing to be kind even when there's nothing in it for us, but that's the heart of our Savior. We imitate God when we demonstrate kindness knowing we'll never be paid back or recognized for it. But God sees it, and that's all that matters.

Kindness Shows Compassion

ACTS 3:1—10 (ESV)

Now Peter and John were going up to the temple at the hour of prayer, the ninth hour. And a man lame from birth was being carried, whom they laid daily at the gate of the temple that is called the Beautiful Gate to ask alms of those entering the temple. Seeing Peter and John about to go into the temple, he asked to receive alms. And Peter directed his gaze at him, as did John, and said, "Look at us." And he fixed his attention on them, expecting to receive something from them. But Peter said, "I have no silver and gold, but what I do have I give to you. In the name of Jesus Christ of Nazareth, rise up and walk!" And he took him by the right hand and raised him up, and immediately his feet and ankles were made strong. And leaping up, he stood and began to walk, and entered the temple with them, walking and leaping and praising God. And all the people saw him walking and praising God, and recognized him as the one who sat at the Beautiful Gate of the temple, asking for alms. And they were filled with wonder and amazement at what had happened to him.

In what circumstances do you tend to feel deep compassion for people?

In this story, how does what the crippled man ask for compare to what he is given?

How does the man immediately respond to his miraculous

healing? How do the people around him respond?

PUT ON A HEART OF *COMPASSION, KINDNESS, HUMILITY, GENTLENESS* AND *PATIENCE.*

— COLOSSIANS 3:12 (NASB)

Think about the people in your life who have needs—whether physical, emotional, or spiritual. How can you compassionately serve them this week? If you'd like, take a moment to pray and ask God to provide opportunities for you to introduce people to Jesus.

YOUR BIGGEST TAKEAWAY

Kindness Provides

Mark 6:34—44 (NASB)

When Jesus went ashore, He saw a large crowd, and He felt compassion for them because they were like sheep without a shepherd; and He began to teach them many things. When it was already quite late, His disciples came to Him and said, "This place is desolate and it is already quite late; send them away so that they may go into the surrounding countryside and villages and buy themselves something to eat." But He answered them, "You give them something to eat!" And they said to Him, "Shall we go and spend two hundred denarii on bread and give them something to eat?" And He said to them, "How many loaves do you have? Go look!" And when they found out, they said, "Five, and two fish." And He commanded them all to sit down by groups on the green grass. They sat down in groups of hundreds and of fifties. And He took the five loaves and the two fish, and looking up toward heaven, He blessed the food and broke the loaves and He kept giving them to the disciples to set before them; and He divided up the two fish among them all. They all ate and were satisfied, and they picked up twelve full baskets of the broken pieces, and also of the fish. There were five thousand men who ate the loaves.

How easy or difficult is it for you to trust that God will provide for your needs?

Why did Jesus have compassion on the crowd of people?
In what ways did He care for them and provide for them?

When Jesus told His disciples to feed the crowd, they were incredulous—it would cost a year's wages to buy enough bread to feed five thousand men (plus women and children). What do you think Jesus wanted to teach His disciples through this miraculous event?

WHEN *GOD'S* PEOPLE ARE IN NEED, BE READY TO *HELP THEM.*

—ROMANS 12:13 (NLT)

What needs do you have right now? Write a prayer, praising God for His love and care for you.

Ask Him to help you to trust Him to provide for you.

_____

_____

_____

_____

_____

_____

_____

_____

_____

_____

_____

_____

_____

_____

_____

_____

YOUR BIGGEST TAKEAWAY

DAY 13

Kindness Restores

MATTHEW 11:25—30 (CEV)

Jesus said:

My Father, Lord of heaven and earth, I am grateful that You hid all this from wise and educated people and showed it to ordinary people. Yes, Father, that is what pleased You.

My Father has given Me everything, and He is the only one who knows the Son. The only one who truly knows the Father is the Son. But the Son wants to tell others about the Father, so that they can know Him too.

If you are tired from carrying heavy burdens, come to Me and I will give you rest. Take the yoke I give you. Put it on your shoulders and learn from Me. I am gentle and humble, and you will find rest. This yoke is easy to bear, and this burden is light.

When have you experienced physical and mental exhaustion? How did you handle it?

What characteristics of Jesus are evident in these verses?

A yoke is a wooden crosspiece placed around the necks of two oxen,

enabling them to share the load in pulling a plow or cart together.

How does this image help you understand Jesus' care for you?

IF YOU ARE TIRED, *JESUS* WILL GIVE YOU *REST.*

In what areas of your life do you need rest and restoration?

What steps will you take to receive the yoke Jesus is offering you?

A NOTE FROM CANDACE

Jesus doesn't want you to crumble under the weight of your physical and emotional stresses, hurts, and weariness. Take your cares to Jesus. Rest in Him. Let Him take the heavy load off you and restore you.

Kindness Is Honorable

Proverbs 3:1–6, 27 (NLT)

My child, never forget the things I have taught you.
   Store my commands in your heart.
If you do this, you will live many years,
   and your life will be satisfying.
Never let loyalty and kindness leave you!
   Tie them around your neck as a reminder.
   Write them deep within your heart.
Then you will find favor with both God and people,
   and you will earn a good reputation.

Trust in the LORD with all your heart;
   do not depend on your own understanding.
Seek His will in all you do,
   and He will show you which path to take. . . .

Do not withhold good from those who deserve it
   when it's in your power to help them.

What are some characteristics of a person who has a good reputation?

How would your friends describe you?

In these verses, what are the characteristics of someone who has an honorable reputation?

What are the benefits we receive when we follow the advice laid out in these proverbs?

How are you already experiencing some of these benefits?

Showing

KINDNESS

honors

God.

What advice in these proverbs is difficult for you to follow? Take a moment to pray and

ask God to guide you as you seek to trust Him and grow in treating people with kindness.

YOUR BIGGEST TAKEAWAY

Kindness Is Rewarded

II Kings 4:8–17 (esv)

One day Elisha went on to Shunem, where a wealthy woman lived, who urged him to eat some food. So whenever he passed that way, he would turn in there to eat food. And she said to her husband, "Behold now, I know that this is a holy man of God who is continually passing our way. Let us make a small room on the roof with walls and put there for him a bed, a table, a chair, and a lamp, so that whenever he comes to us, he can go in there."

One day he came there, and he turned into the chamber and rested there. And he said to Gehazi his servant, "Call this Shunammite." When he had called her, she stood before him. And he said to him, "Say now to her, 'See, you have taken all this trouble for us; what is to be done for you? Would you have a word spoken on your behalf to the king or to the commander of the army?'" She answered, "I dwell among my own people." And he said, "What then is to be done for her?" Gehazi answered, "Well, she has no son, and her husband is old." He said, "Call her." And when he had called her, she stood in the doorway. And he said, "At this season, about this time next year, you shall embrace a son." And she said, "No, my lord, O man of God; do not lie to your servant." But the woman conceived, and she bore a son about that time the following spring, as Elisha had said to her.

What motivates you to show kindness toward people?

How does the woman show kindness to the prophet Elisha?

What do you think motivated her kindness?

What does God do for the woman of Shunem because of her kindness to Elisha?

Your
kindness
will
REWARD YOU.

— Proverbs 11:17 (NLT)

God sees our hearts and knows what motivates us in how we treat people.

In what ways has He rewarded you for your selfless acts of kindness?

What do you think is the ultimate reward for showing kindness?

YOUR BIGGEST TAKEAWAY

Kindness
Is Respectful

I Timothy 5:1–8 (GNT)

Do not rebuke an older man, but appeal to him as if he were your father. Treat the younger men as your brothers, the older women as mothers, and the younger women as sisters, with all purity.

Show respect for widows who really are all alone. But if a widow has children or grandchildren, they should learn first to carry out their religious duties toward their own family and in this way repay their parents and grandparents, because that is what pleases God. A widow who is all alone, with no one to take care of her, has placed her hope in God and continues to pray and ask Him for His help night and day. But a widow who gives herself to pleasure has already died, even though she lives. Give them these instructions, so that no one will find fault with them. But if any do not take care of their relatives, especially the members of their own family, they have denied the faith and are worse than an unbeliever.

In what ways are you setting a good example in showing respect to members of your family or people in your community?

According to the apostle Paul, who wrote I Timothy, how should we treat older people? How should we treat younger people?

What responsibilities do we have to care for widows?
What responsibilities do we have to care for our relatives?

LOVE ONE ANOTHER *WARMLY . . .* SHOW *RESPECT* FOR ONE ANOTHER.

— ROMANS 12:10 (GNT)

Sadly, many elderly people are neglected by their families or left alone by their communities.

How can you reach out to an elderly person with respect and kindness this week?

_____

_____

_____

_____

_____

_____

_____

_____

_____

_____

_____

_____

_____

_____

A NOTE FROM CANDACE

Even though I didn't grow up in a Christian home, I'm thankful my parents taught me the value of showing kindness, respect, and love to everyone—no matter who they are. Jesus is the perfect example we can follow for showing kindness and respect.

Kindness Protects

PSALM 31:1–5, 21 (NKJV)

In You, O LORD, I put my trust;

Let me never be ashamed;

Deliver me in Your righteousness.

Bow down Your ear to me,

Deliver me speedily;

Be my rock of refuge,

A fortress of defense to save me.

For You are my rock and my fortress;

Therefore, for Your name's sake,

Lead me and guide me.

Pull me out of the net which they have secretly laid for me,

For You are my strength.

Into Your hand I commit my spirit;

You have redeemed me, O LORD God of truth. . . .

Blessed be the LORD,

For He has shown me His marvelous kindness in a strong city!

Who do you turn to when you feel vulnerable and need protection?

Israel's King David experienced times of fear and vulnerability.

In this psalm, what does David ask God to do for him?

According to these verses, how has God shown kindness

to David, and how does David respond?

GOD
IS MY ROCK AND
MY FORTRESS.

How has God shown kindness to you in the ways He's protected you and shielded you from harm? In what current circumstances do you need to trust Him to provide strength and protection?

YOUR BIGGEST TAKEAWAY

Kindness Brings Joy

JEREMIAH 31:3—6 (NIV)

[The people of Israel had rebelled against God and had been exiled from their land as a consequence. Yet because of His love for them, God promised to restore them:]

"I have loved you with an everlasting love;
    I have drawn you with unfailing kindness.
I will build you up again,
    and you, Virgin Israel, will be rebuilt.
Again you will take up your timbrels
    and go out to dance with the joyful.
Again you will plant vineyards
    on the hills of Samaria;
the farmers will plant them
    and enjoy their fruit.
There will be a day when watchmen cry out
    on the hills of Ephraim,
'Come, let us go up to Zion,
    to the LORD our God.'"

How does receiving undeserved kindness from someone make you feel? How do you respond?

The people of Israel didn't do anything to deserve God's love or kindness, yet God faithfully loved them and fulfilled His promises to them. What promises does God give His people in these verses?

How will the people respond to God's kindness toward them?

He has shown *KINDNESS . . .* AND FILLS YOUR HEARTS WITH *JOY.*

— ACTS 14:17 (NIV)

What promises in the Bible do you hold on to when you're struggling to find joy?

How has the kindness of God brought joy into your life?

_____

_____

_____

_____

_____

_____

_____

_____

_____

_____

_____

_____

_____

_____

YOUR BIGGEST TAKEAWAY

Kindness Endures

II Corinthians 6:1—10 (CEV)

We [Paul and his companions] work together with God, and we beg you [the Christians in Corinth] to make good use of God's kindness to you. . . . That time has come. This is the day for you to be saved.

We don't want anyone to find fault with our work, and so we try hard not to cause problems. But in everything and in every way we show that we truly are God's servants. We have always been patient, though we have had a lot of trouble, suffering, and hard times. We have been beaten, put in jail, and hurt in riots. We have worked hard and have gone without sleep or food. But we have kept ourselves pure and have been understanding, patient, and kind. The Holy Spirit has been with us, and our love has been real. We have spoken the truth, and God's power has worked in us. In all our struggles we have said and done only what is right.

Whether we were honored or dishonored or praised or cursed, we always told the truth about ourselves. But some people said we did not. We are unknown to others, but well known to you. We seem to be dying, and yet we are still alive. We have been punished, but never killed, and we are always happy, even in times of suffering. Although we are poor, we have made many people rich. And though we own nothing, everything is ours.

When have you received criticism for doing what you believed was the right thing to do?

What hardships did Paul and his companions endure while they worked

and traveled to bring God's message of salvation to people?

How does Paul describe himself and his companions in these verses?

What role does the Holy Spirit play in Paul's work?

LOVE
is kind
and
PATIENT.

— I CORINTHIANS 13:4 (CEV)

How do these verses encourage you to endure in your faith? In what ways can you patiently treat people with kindness this week—even if they criticize or falsely accuse you?

_____
_____
_____
_____
_____
_____
_____
_____
_____
_____
_____
_____
_____
_____
_____

A NOTE FROM CANDACE

I'm often criticized—it's part of being in the public eye. It used to really weigh me down, but I've come to realize that I'll never please everyone. I *can* choose to patiently endure and show kindness in every circumstance. And you know what? I've never regretted being kind to my critics.

DAY 20

Kindness Brings Hope

PSALM 145:13–20 (NLT)

The LORD always keeps His promises;

   He is gracious in all He does.

The LORD helps the fallen

   and lifts those bent beneath their loads.

The eyes of all look to You in hope;

   You give them their food as they need it.

When You open Your hand,

   You satisfy the hunger and thirst of every living thing.

The LORD is righteous in everything He does;

   He is filled with kindness.

The LORD is close to all who call on Him,

   yes, to all who call on Him in truth.

He grants the desires of those who fear Him;

   He hears their cries for help and rescues them.

The LORD protects all those who love Him,

   but He destroys the wicked.

What hope do you have for your future? What is that hope based on?

How is God described in these verses?

Which characteristics of God in these verses cause you to praise Him?

Which bring you comfort and hope?

GOD OUR FATHER

. . . IS KIND AND HAS GIVEN US ETERNAL

COMFORT

AND A WONDERFUL

HOPE.

—II THESSALONIANS 2:16 (CEV)

Why is it important to place your hope in God and not in anything or anyone else?

If you'd like, write down a prayer of praise, thanking God for keeping

His promises and for giving you every reason to have hope.

_____

_____

_____

_____

_____

_____

_____

_____

_____

_____

_____

_____

_____

_____

YOUR BIGGEST TAKEAWAY

105

Kindness Brings Healing

LUKE 5:12–13; 7:11–16 (CSB)

While [Jesus] was in one of the towns, a man was there who had leprosy all over him. He saw Jesus, fell facedown, and begged Him, "Lord, if You are willing, You can make me clean."

Reaching out His hand, Jesus touched him, saying, "I am willing; be made clean," and immediately the leprosy left him. . . .

Afterward He was on His way to a town called Nain. His disciples and a large crowd were traveling with Him. Just as He neared the gate of the town, a dead man was being carried out. He was his mother's only son, and she was a widow. A large crowd from the city was also with her. When the Lord saw her, He had compassion on her and said, "Don't weep." Then He came up and touched the open coffin, and the pallbearers stopped. And He said, "Young man, I tell you, get up!"

The dead man sat up and began to speak, and Jesus gave him to his mother. Then fear came over everyone, and they glorified God, saying, "A great prophet has risen among us," and "God has visited His people."

How has someone's kind words or actions brought healing

in your life—whether emotionally, spiritually, or relationally?

In these two stories, how does Jesus demonstrate kindness?

How do the people from Nain respond to Jesus' raising of the dead man?

HAVE COMPASSION ON ME, *LORD* . . . HEAL ME.

— PSALM 6:2 (NLT)

How have you responded in the past to God's work of healing in your life?

Write down all the ways you have experienced His healing.

Then take a moment to praise Him for His kindness toward you.

_____
_____
_____
_____
_____
_____
_____
_____
_____
_____
_____
_____
_____

YOUR BIGGEST TAKEAWAY

Kindness Overcomes Shame

Isaiah 54:4—8, 10 (NIV)

"Do not be afraid; you will not be put to shame.

    Do not fear disgrace; you will not be humiliated.

You will forget the shame of your youth . . .

    The LORD will call you back

    as if you were a wife deserted and distressed in spirit—

a wife who married young,

    only to be rejected," says your God.

"For a brief moment I abandoned you,

    but with deep compassion I will bring you back.

In a surge of anger

    I hid My face from you for a moment,

but with everlasting kindness

    I will have compassion on you,"

    says the LORD your Redeemer. . . .

"Though the mountains be shaken

    and the hills be removed,

yet My unfailing love for you will not be shaken."

How do feelings of shame keep us from growing

in our relationships with God and with other people?

In these verses, how does God comfort His people,

who had rejected Him and sinned against Him?

What do you learn about God from these verses?

GOD'S

UNFAILING LOVE FOR YOU WILL NOT BE SHAKEN.

When have you felt that God would abandon you because of your

shameful thoughts, words, or actions? What encouragement can you receive from these verses,

and how can you share God's love with others who may be struggling with shame?

_____

_____

_____

_____

_____

_____

_____

_____

_____

_____

_____

_____

_____

A NOTE FROM CANDACE

We all make mistakes. We all have moments from our pasts we're not proud of. But God wants to set us free from shame. He loves us and won't abandon us. Let's follow His lead by offering kindness and forgiveness when others mess up.

DAY 23

Kindness
Brings Unity

ROMANS 15:1—9 (CEV)

If our faith is strong, we should be patient with the Lord's followers whose faith is weak. We should try to please them instead of ourselves. We should think of their good and try to help them by doing what pleases them. Even Christ did not try to please Himself. But as the Scriptures say, "The people who insulted You also insulted Me." And the Scriptures were written to teach and encourage us by giving us hope. God is the one who makes us patient and cheerful. I pray that He will help you live at peace with each other, as you follow Christ. Then all of you together will praise God, the Father of our Lord Jesus Christ.

Honor God by accepting each other, as Christ has accepted you. I tell you that Christ came as a servant of the Jews to show that God has kept the promises He made to their famous ancestors. Christ also came, so that the Gentiles would praise God for being kind to them.

In what ways do you think patience and peace are connected?

What specific instructions does Paul, the author of Romans,
give to Jesus' followers whose "faith is strong"?

Based on these verses, how can followers of Jesus work to
develop unity and peace among themselves?

LIVE

PEACEFULLY

WITH EACH OTHER.

— I THESSALONIANS 5:13 (NLT)

What steps can you take to show more kindness in situations where you struggle with impatience?

How can you intentionally work to foster peace in your relationships with people?

_____

_____

_____

_____

_____

_____

_____

_____

_____

_____

_____

_____

YOUR BIGGEST TAKEAWAY

Kindness Has No Limits

MARK 2:2–12 (NLT)

The house where [Jesus] was staying was so packed with visitors that there was no more room, even outside the door. While He was preaching God's word to them, four men arrived carrying a paralyzed man on a mat. They couldn't bring him to Jesus because of the crowd, so they dug a hole through the roof above His head. Then they lowered the man on his mat, right down in front of Jesus. Seeing their faith, Jesus said to the paralyzed man, "My child, your sins are forgiven."

But some of the teachers of religious law who were sitting there thought to themselves, "What is He saying? This is blasphemy! Only God can forgive sins!"

Jesus knew immediately what they were thinking, so He asked them, "Why do you question this in your hearts? Is it easier to say to the paralyzed man 'Your sins are forgiven,' or 'Stand up, pick up your mat, and walk'? So I will prove to you that the Son of Man has the authority on earth to forgive sins." Then Jesus turned to the paralyzed man and said, "Stand up, pick up your mat, and go home!"

And the man jumped up, grabbed his mat, and walked out through the stunned onlookers. They were all amazed and praised God, exclaiming, "We've never seen anything like this before!"

Do you have a friend who is struggling through a difficult situation?

What help are you willing to offer your friend?

How would you describe the paralyzed man's four friends based on their

actions in this story? What does Jesus notice about them?

How does Jesus respond when He sees the faith of the paralyzed man's friends?

What kindness does He show the paralyzed man?

THE GREATEST THING
A MAN CAN DO FOR
HIS HEAVENLY

FATHER

IS TO BE KIND TO
SOME OF HIS OTHER

CHILDREN.

— HENRY DRUMMOND